Coins

Bank notes   Postage stamps

Compass

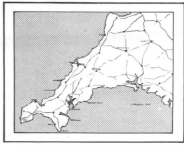

Map

Weather-vane

$$1,0\,0\,0 = a \quad thousand$$

$$1,0\,0\,0,0\,0\,0 = a \quad million$$

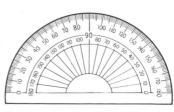

Ruler

Protractor

Thermometer   Angle

Series 661

The authors of the Ladybird 'Words for Number' Series are authorities on the teaching of reading, and joint authors of the research work — 'Key Words to Literacy' published by The Schoolmaster Publishing Co. Ltd.

W. Murray is an experienced headmaster and lecturer, and is author of the Ladybird Key Words Reading Scheme. J. McNally, recently engaged on further research work, was Chief Educational Psychologist to Manchester Education Committee.

Book 4

THE LADYBIRD
WORDS FOR NUMBER SERIES

Everyday words for Numbers

Revised for Metrication

by
J. McNALLY and W. MURRAY
(Authors of 'Key Words to Literacy')

with illustrations by
KENNETH INNS

Publishers; Wills & Hepworth Ltd., Loughborough
First published 1967   ©   Printed in England

coins   new penny   piece

1. Here are three coins, a $\frac{1}{2}$ new
    penny, a new penny and a 2
    new pence piece.

2. Two $\frac{1}{2}$ new pennies are worth
    one new penny.

    $\frac{1}{2}p + \frac{1}{2}p = 1p$

3. Two new pennies are worth a
    2 new pence piece.

    $1p + 1p = 2p$

How many $\frac{1}{2}$ new pennies would
make a 2 new pence piece?

A 50 new pence
piece is worth five 10 new pence pieces

A pound note is worth
two 50 new pence pieces

coins actual size

A five pound note is worth five one pound notes

**Post Office   postage stamps
postal orders   money orders
exchange Savings Bank form**

1. A Post Office sells postage stamps for letters and parcels.

2. It sells postal orders and money orders and it also exchanges these for money. Instead of sending real money by post, it is safer to buy a postal order (or a money order) and send this by post.

3. You may keep money in a Post Office Savings Bank. The money you pay in is entered in your Post Office Savings book.

4. To take out some of your money, you fill in a form and sign it.

2

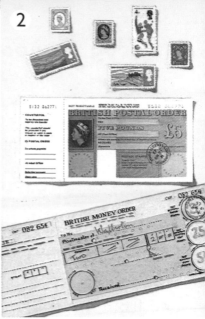

4

POST OFFICE
SAVINGS
BANK

BARNHAM
BOGNOR REGIS

№ 1633

Quote the above particulars on all
letters to the Savings Department
and on all withdrawal forms

STATE SECURITY

midday   noon   midnight
hours   a.m.   p.m.

There are seven days in a week. There are twenty-four hours in each day. The middle of the day is called midday or noon, or twelve o'clock, daytime.

There is also a twelve o'clock at night, and this is called midnight.

From midnight to midday is twelve hours, and from midday to the next midnight is another twelve hours. These two twelves make up one full day of twenty-four hours.

When we tell the time in any one day we put a.m. after the hours from midnight until midday. For example, eight o'clock in the morning is 8 a.m.

We put p.m. after the hours from midday to midnight. Thus eight o'clock in the evening is 8 p.m.

---

a.m. means ante meridiem (before midday)
p.m. means post meridiem (after midday)

School time.
It is 9 a.m.

It is noon, or
12 o'clock midday.

Bedtime.
It is 9 p.m.

It is 12 o'clock
midnight.

minutes   seconds   watch

On a clock face the hour hand moves right round once in the day and once in the night (i.e. twice in 24 hours).

In each hour there are 60 minutes. It takes about an hour for some children to get up from bed, wash, dress, have breakfast and walk to school.

A minute is not a long time. The seconds hand on a watch or clock moves round in a full circle once in a minute. A second is a very short time. You can speak about three or four words in one second. There are 60 seconds in one minute.

When telling the time, the twenty-four hour clock is sometimes used. The hour after twelve o'clock noon is not then called 1 p.m., but 13.00 hours instead. Two o'clock in the afternoon is called 14.00 hours, and so on until midnight— which is called 24.00 hours.

The hour hand moves right round the clock face twice in a day and night (i.e. 24 hours).

The minute hand moves round the clock face in one hour (i.e. 60 minutes).

The seconds hand moves round the small circle once in a minute (i.e. 60 seconds).

This is 8 a.m. in the morning or 8 p.m. in the evening. By the 24 hour clock the time would be 08.00 hours or 20.00 hours.

sum   **difference**   **product**

division   **quotient**   **remainder**

divisor   **dividend**

1. One boy has 4 marbles and the other has 5. The sum total of marbles is 9.

   When we add up, the answer is called the sum.

2. The boy gives away 3 from his 9 marbles. The difference between the number he had first and the number he gave away is 6.

   If we take a number away from a larger one, the amount remaining is the difference.

3. There are 3 rows of milk bottles with 4 bottles in each row.

   The answer when two numbers are multiplied together is the product.

4. In a division sum the answer is called the quotient, and any number left over is the remainder. The number we divide by is the divisor. The dividend is the number which is divided up.

The sum of
5 and 4
is 9

$$\begin{array}{r} 5 \\ +4 \\ \hline 9 \end{array}$$

The difference between 9 and 3 is 6

$$\begin{array}{r} 9 \\ -3 \\ \hline 6 \end{array}$$

When 4 is multiplied by 3 the product is 12

$$\begin{array}{r} 4 \\ \times 3 \\ \hline 12 \end{array}$$

divisor →

$$\begin{array}{r} 2 \leftarrow \text{quotient} \\ 4 \overline{)9} \leftarrow \text{dividend} \\ 8 \\ \hline 1 \leftarrow \text{remainder} \end{array}$$

parts   twice   size   fourth
fraction   third   vulgar fractions

1. The four boys have a whole melon. They divide it into four equal parts. They cut it first into two halves and then into quarters. A whole melon is twice the size of half of it.

   Each boy has a quarter. A quarter is a fourth part of the whole. We write a quarter as $\frac{1}{4}$.

   Another name for a part of a whole is a fraction. $\frac{1}{4}$ is a fraction of the whole melon.

   How many quarters in one? There are four. We could write this as

   $$1 = \frac{1}{4} + \frac{1}{4} + \frac{1}{4} + \frac{1}{4}.$$

2. The three girls have a cake to share beween them. Each has an equal part. They have a third of the cake each. A third is written $\frac{1}{3}$. $\frac{1}{3}$ is a fraction of the whole cake. We could write this as $1 = \frac{1}{3} + \frac{1}{3} + \frac{1}{3}$.

   These fractions are called vulgar fractions.

An introduction to decimal fractions

The decimal system is a system of counting based on tens.

It uses the decimal point, which is a dot placed after the unit figure. The first figure to the right of the decimal point means tenths of one.

For example—

·1 means $\frac{1}{10}$ of one

·5 means $\frac{5}{10}$ of one

·7 means $\frac{7}{10}$ of one

The second figure after the decimal point means hundredths (e.g. ·03 = $\frac{3}{100}$), and the third figure after the decimal point means thousandths (e.g. ·007 = $\frac{7}{1000}$).

Example—

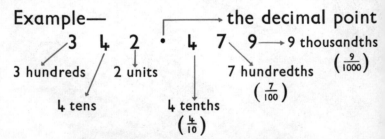

decimal fractions

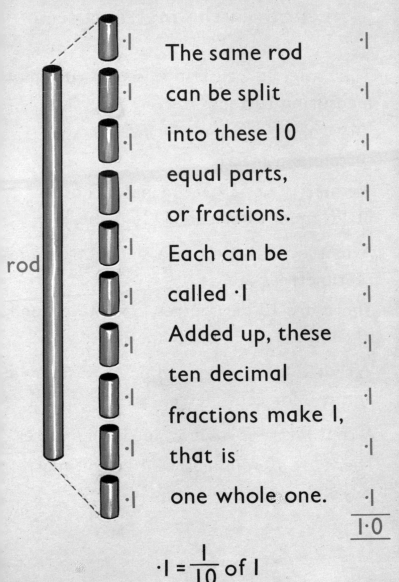

rod

The same rod
can be split
into these 10
equal parts,
or fractions.
Each can be
called ·1
Added up, these
ten decimal
fractions make 1,
that is
one whole one.

·1
·1
·1
·1
·1
·1
·1
·1
·1
·1
_____
1·0

$$·1 = \frac{1}{10} \text{ of } 1$$

Length in the metric system

The metric system is a decimal measuring system.

The unit of length in the metric system is a metre.

A metre is 39·37 inches. That is a little longer than a yard (36 inches).

A metre is divided into decimetres and centimetres.

There are 10 decimetres in a metre, and 10 centimetres in a decimetre.

We write m. for metre, dm. for decimetre and cm. for centimetre.

A centimetre is divided into millimetres.

There are 10 millimetres in a centimetre.

We write mm. for millimetre.

One yard (3 feet or 36 inches)

One metre (39·37 inches)

This picture shows part of a ruler
(actual size) marked in millimetres,
centimetres and inches

metres   mile   thousand   million

1. On sports days there are short races such as 100 metres and 200 metres, and longer races such as 1000 metres, 1500 metres and one mile.

> A mile is 1,760 yards
> 1500 metres is 1,640 yards
> 1000 metres = 1 kilometre
>   (1000 m. = 1 km.)
> A kilometre is approximately $\frac{5}{8}$ of a mile.

2. A thousand is ten hundreds. A very big factory can employ several thousand workers.

3. A million is a thousand thousands. We write 1,000,000 for a million. There are millions of grains of sand on the beach.

angles   protractor

1. When two straight lines meet they form one or more angles.

2. An angle is sometimes described as the amount of turning of a line from one position to another. The *amount* of turning is measured in degrees. This angle shows a turning amount of 90 degrees. We write this as 90°.

3. Here is an angle of 120°.

4. This angle is 45°.

5. This is a protractor being used to measure an angle. The bottom line on the protractor is put along one of the straight lines forming the angle. The middle point of the line on the protractor is put at the point on the paper where the straight lines join. The angle is read where the second line on the paper cuts the half circle on the protractor, reading up from the 0.

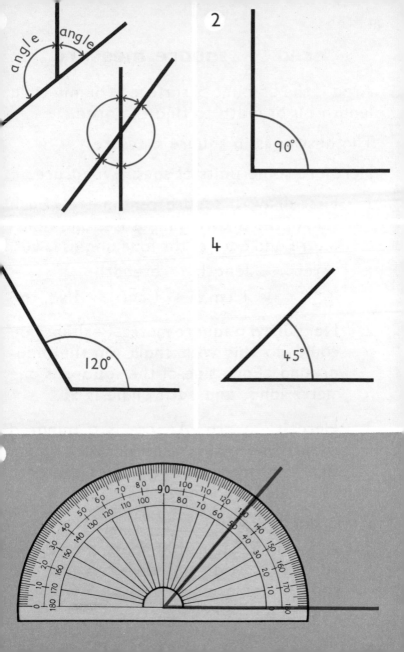

area   square measure

Area is the amount of surface. You multiply length by breadth to find the area.

The answer is in square measure.

Here are some units of square measure.

1. First draw a square centimetre. Each side of the drawing measures one centimetre and each of the four angles is 90°.

    Area = length × breadth

         = 1 cm. × 1 cm. = 1 sq. cm.

2. Next draw a square metre. Perhaps you could do this with chalk, on the playground. Each side of the square is one metre long, and each angle is 90°.

3. Here is an are. An are is a hundred square metres. In the drawing, each side is 10 metres. The angles are each 90°, called right angles.

4. A dekare is 10 ares.

    A football pitch 100 metres long by 50 metres wide has an area of 5,000 square metres or 50 ares or 5 dekares.

The area of the
figure drawn is
One square centimetre
(1 sq.cm)
(actual size)

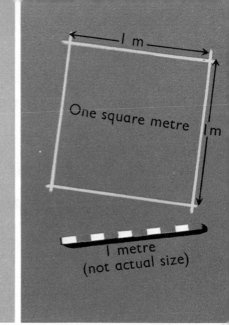

One square metre

1 metre
(not actual size)

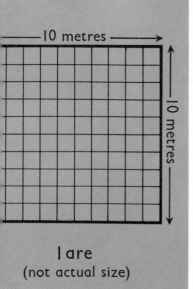

10 metres

10 metres

1 are
(not actual size)

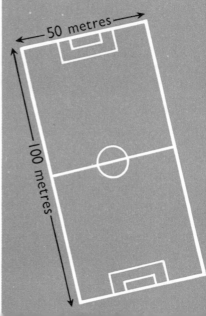

50 metres

100 metres

volume   capacity
cubic centimetre
litre   pint   container

Volume, or capacity, is easily found if you can measure the length, breadth and depth of an object. You multiply the three together to find the volume.

The answer is given in cubic measure.

1. A container measuring a cubic decimetre (1000 cubic centimetres) holds one litre.

2. A litre is about $1\frac{3}{4}$ pints.

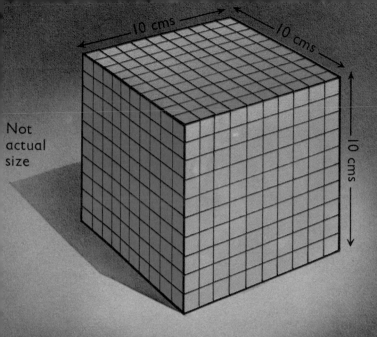

Not actual size

10 cms — 10 cms — 10 cms

10×10×10 cms =1000 cubic centimetres =1 litre

a pint   a litre

Metric weight
gram   kilogram

The unit of weight in the metric system is the gram. It is exactly the weight of—

One cubic centimetre of water.

(A $\frac{1}{2}$ new penny weighs about $1\frac{3}{4}$ grams).

A kilogram is 1000 grams.

(A kilogram is about $2\frac{1}{4}$ pounds weight).

1 pound (or 16 ounces) is equal to 454 grams.

a cubic centimetre

One cubic centimetre of water weighs 1 gram

1 c.c. of water weighs 1 gram

1 Kilogram   2·2005 lbs

map   compass

North   South   East   West

N.   S.   E.   W.   scale

The boys and girls are out for a long walk. They have a map and a compass to help them find the way.

The needle of the compass always points to the north. They line up the map with the compass so that they know which is north, south, east and west on the map.

They know the scale of the map is one inch to a mile. Every inch on the map means one mile on the ground. The map shows $4\frac{1}{2}$ inches of road they have to travel. This means they have to go $4\frac{1}{2}$ miles.

There is a weather-vane in the picture. It turns as the wind blows.

It has N for north, S for south, E for east and W for west. The arrow on the weather-vane points to the west. This means that the wind is blowing from the west.

seasons **Spring** **Summer**
Autumn **Winter** **weather**

The year has four seasons. They are Spring, Summer, Autumn and Winter.

1. Spring follows Winter. It is less cold in Spring. Leaves and flowers start to grow.

   Birds sing and build their nests.

2. The hot season of Summer comes after Spring. The trees are green and there are very many birds and flowers. People play outdoor games and bathe in the sea.

3. Autumn follows Summer. The weather is colder. Fruit is picked and leaves and flowers begin to die.

4. Winter comes next. The days are shorter and very cold. The trees are bare and there is rain and sometimes snow.

Spring

Summer

Autumn

Winter

temperature   thermometer

degrees   cold   low   hot   high

When the weather is warm we say that the temperature is high. When it is cold the temperature is low.

We measure temperature with a thermometer. The thermometer is marked in degrees.

---

1. It is a hot summer day. The sun is shining. A thermometer would show that the temperature is high.

2. It is winter. There is ice and snow. The thermometer would show that the temperature is very low.

3. The water in the kettle is very hot. The temperature of the water is very high.

4. The boy is ill. He feels hot. The nurse takes his temperature with a thermometer and finds that it is high.

Centigrade scale   freezing point boiling point   expands   contracts

Water always boils at the same temperature. Water always freezes at the same temperature. These two facts have been used to make scales for measuring temperature. One of these scales is called the Centigrade scale.

On this scale the exact point at which water freezes is called 0 degrees Centigrade, and the point at which it boils is called 100 degrees Centigrade. We write these as 0°C and 100°C.

A silver-coloured liquid called mercury is put into a thin tube. The mercury expands as the temperature increases and contracts as the temperature falls.

The length of the tube between the freezing point and the boiling point is divided into 100 equal spaces. Each space is called one degree. Thus 50 degrees (or 50°C.) is halfway between the freezing point and the boiling point of water.

Fahrenheit scale   measurement

Another scale for measuring temperature is called the Fahrenheit Scale. On this, freezing point is marked as 32 degrees Fahrenheit, and boiling point as 212 degrees Fahrenheit. These are written as 32°F, and 212°F. Thus there are 180° between these two points on the Fahrenheit scale.

Many thermometers show both the Fahrenheit and the Centigrade scales. On these thermometers you can compare a Fahrenheit measurement with a Centigrade measurement. For example, when the temperature on a hot day in summer is 77° Fahrenheit, then the Centigrade thermometer reading is 25°.

To take another example. On a colder day, when the Fahrenheit reading is 50°, then the Centigrade temperature is 10°.

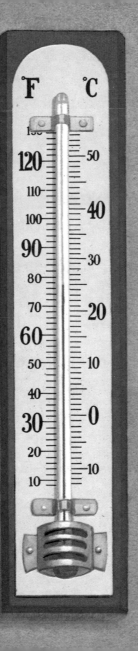

distance   speed

Sometimes we move slowly and sometimes quickly. We walk more slowly than we cycle. We drive in a car more quickly than we cycle. A racing car goes very fast. An aeroplane goes fastest of all.

When we go a long distance in a short time, we move at a high speed. We measure speed in kilometres or miles an hour.

A kilometre is approximately $\frac{5}{8}$ of a mile. 8 kilometres may be regarded as 5 miles.

1. If an aeroplane flies at 500 miles an hour, this is about 800 kilometres an hour.

2. If a racing car travels at 100 miles an hour, this is about 160 kilometres an hour.

**compass   centre   circumference
radius   diameter   semi-circle
pattern**

Have you a pair of compasses and a pencil? Draw a circle on a piece of paper.

The hole made by the compass point is at the centre of the circle. The long continuous line drawn to make the circle is called the circumference.

A straight line from the centre to the circumference is a radius of the circle.

A straight line drawn right across the circle, going through the centre point, is called a diameter. A diameter is twice the length of a radius.

The diameter divides the circle into two semi-circles.

You can draw another circle, and make a pattern in it, using compasses and pencil.

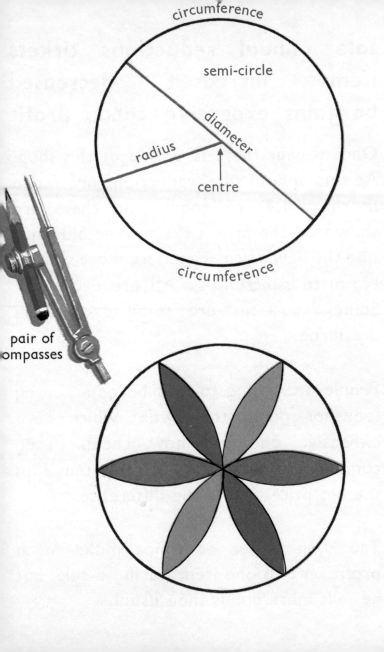

circumference

semi-circle

diameter

radius

centre

circumference

pair of compasses

sale annual reductions tickets items increased decreased bargains expensive cheap profit

Once a year there is a sale at this shop. At this annual sale, reductions are made in the prices of goods and these are shown on the price tickets. The old price and the new price of each item are shown. No price is increased. All are decreased. Some reductions are small and others are large.

People are trying to find bargains. They look for goods they want which were expensive and are now cheap. They compare the new price of each item with the old price to find the difference.

The shop owner does not make much profit on any one item during a sale, but he sells more goods than usual.

Imperial Units

Measurement of Length

12 inches	=	1 foot
3 feet	=	1 yard
22 yards	=	1 chain
10 chains	=	1 furlong
8 furlongs	=	1 mile
1,760 yards	=	1 mile

Measurement of Area

144 square inches	=	1 square foot
9 square feet	=	1 square yard
1,210 square yards	=	1 rood
4 roods	=	1 acre
4,840 square yards	=	1 acre
640 acres	=	1 square mile

Measurement of Volume

1,728 cubic inches	=	1 cubic foot
27 cubic feet	=	1 cubic yard

Measurement of Capacity

4 gills	=	1 pint
2 pints	=	1 quart
4 quarts	=	1 gallon
2 gallons	=	1 peck
4 pecks	=	1 bushel
8 bushels	=	1 quarter

Measurement of Weight

16 drams	=	1 ounce
16 ounces	=	1 pound
14 pounds	=	1 stone
28 pounds	=	1 quarter
4 quarters	=	1 hundredweight
20 hundredweights	=	1 ton
2,240 pounds	=	1 ton